Theory Paper Grade 3 2018 A
Model Answers

1   (10)

2   (10)

(a)

or

(b) twelve

3   (10)

or

4 E major   (10)

F melodic minor

A major

C harmonic minor

5   (10)

6  (10)

7 (10)

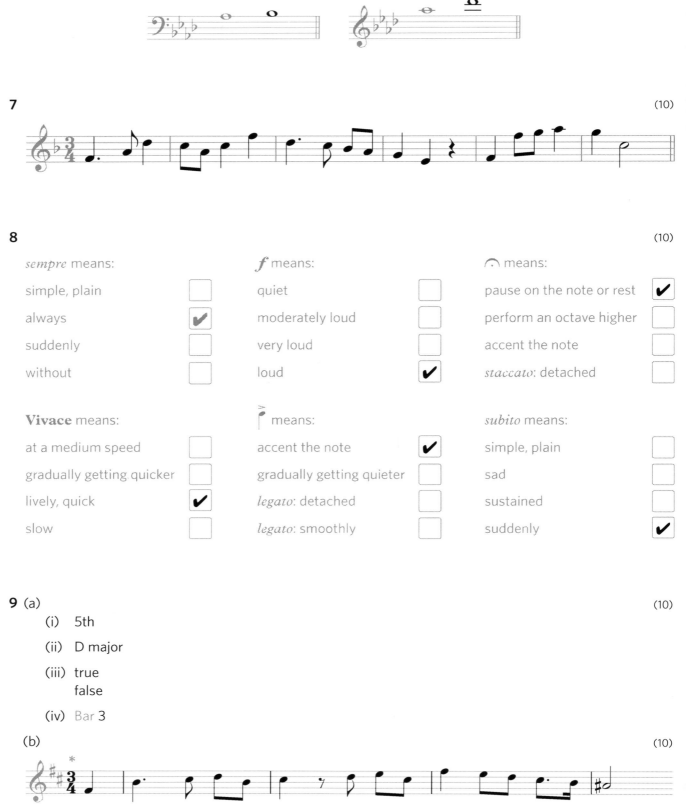

8 (10)

sempre means:			*f* means:			⌒ means:	
simple, plain	☐		quiet	☐		pause on the note or rest	✔
always	✔		moderately loud	☐		perform an octave higher	☐
suddenly	☐		very loud	☐		accent the note	☐
without	☐		loud	✔		*staccato*: detached	☐

Vivace means:			˃ means:			*subito* means:	
at a medium speed	☐		accent the note	✔		simple, plain	☐
gradually getting quicker	☐		gradually getting quieter	☐		sad	☐
lively, quick	✔		*legato*: detached	☐		sustained	☐
slow	☐		*legato*: smoothly	☐		suddenly	✔

9 (a) (10)

    (i)   5th

    (ii)   D major

    (iii) true
            false

    (iv) Bar 3

  (b) (10)

Theory Paper   Grade 3   2018   B
Model Answers

1 (10)

2 (10)

3 (10)
(a)
(b)

or
or

4   G sharp   A / A natural   D sharp   (10)
    A flat   B flat   C / C natural

5 (10)

6 (10)

7 (10)

8 (10)

p means:

moderately loud	☐
very loud	☐
very quiet	☐
quiet	✔

Largo means:

slow, stately	✔
rather slow	☐
smoothly	☐
at a medium speed	☐

⌒ means:

slur: detached	☐
slur: perform smoothly	✔
tie: detached	☐
tie: hold for the value of both notes	☐

leggiero means:

light	✔
graceful	☐
smoothly	☐
rather slow	☐

⎺ means:

sforzando	☐
staccatissimo	☐
strong accent	☐
slight pressure	✔

8ᵛᵃ⎺⎺⌉ means:

perform an octave higher	✔
perform an octave lower	☐
perform the notes smoothly	☐
pause on the note or rest	☐

9 (a) (10)

(i) 6th

(ii) simple quadruple

(iii) three

(iv) false

(v)

(b) (10)

Theory Paper   Grade 3   2018   C
Model Answers

5   major   major   perfect   (10)
        7th   2nd   octave / 8ve / 8th

          perfect   minor
           5th   3rd

6   C♯ minor   B minor   E♭ major   (10)

          F minor   D major

7   (10)

(a)

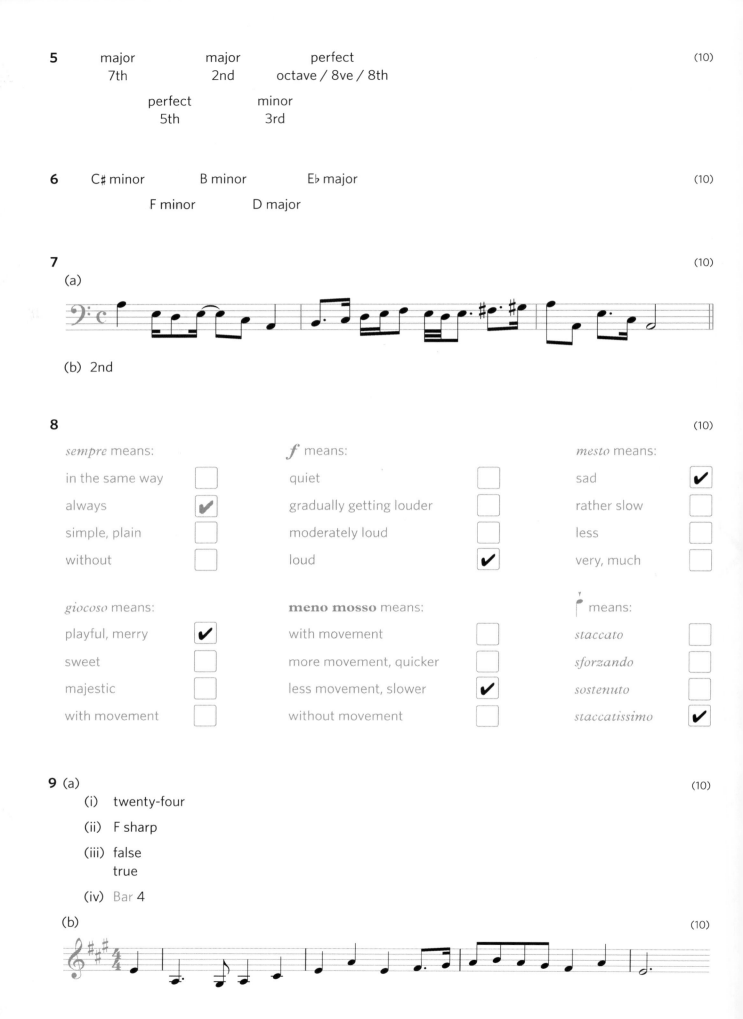

(b) 2nd

8   (10)

sempre means:		*f* means:		*mesto* means:	
in the same way		quiet		sad	✔
always	✔	gradually getting louder		rather slow	
simple, plain		moderately loud		less	
without		loud	✔	very, much	

giocoso means:		**meno mosso** means:		˘ means:	
playful, merry	✔	with movement		*staccato*	
sweet		more movement, quicker		*sforzando*	
majestic		less movement, slower	✔	*sostenuto*	
with movement		without movement		*staccatissimo*	✔

9 (a)   (10)

      (i)   twenty-four

      (ii) F sharp

      (iii) false
           true

      (iv) Bar 4

(b)   (10)

Model Answers

1   (10)

2   (10)

(a)

(b)   simple

quadruple

3   major   major   perfect   (10)
      2nd   7th   4th

           minor   perfect
           6th   octave / 8ve / 8th

4   (10)

5   (10)

6

G sharp	B flat	A / A natural
F sharp	E flat	D / D natural

7 (10)

or

or

8 (10)

mp means:

moderately quick	☐
very quiet	☐
loud	☐
moderately quiet	☑

subito means:

suddenly	☑
sad	☐
sustained	☐
always	☐

marcato means:

emphatic, accented	☑
in a military style	☐
majestic	☐
very slow, solemn	☐

scherzando means:

simple, plain	☐
playful, joking	☑
spirited	☐
forced, accented	☐

❛ means:

staccato: detached	☑
legato: detached	☐
accent the note	☐
staccato: smoothly	☐

cantabile means:

repeat from the beginning	☐
in a singing style	☑
slow	☐
smoothly	☐

9 (a) (10)

  (i)   5th

  (ii) true

  (iii) B flat

  (iv) ten

  (v)   two / two crotchets / two quarter notes / one minim / one half note / one beat

  (b) (10)